For Ian + Irene with great affection
and to show you our roots!
3.10.1997   Michael + Mary

DERBYSHIRE

A portrait in colour

BILL MEADOWS & WILLIAM AMOS

COUNTRYSIDE BOOKS

Other counties in this series include:

BUCKINGHAMSHIRE	ESSEX
CHESHIRE	HAMPSHIRE
DEVON	SUFFOLK
DORSET	SURREY

SUSSEX

First Published 1995
© Photographs, Bill Meadows 1995
© Text, William Amos 1995

COUNTRYSIDE BOOKS
3 CATHERINE ROAD
NEWBURY, BERKSHIRE

ISBN 1 85306 331 2

Produced through MRM Associates Ltd., Reading
Typeset by Paragon Typesetters, Queensferry, Clwyd
Printed in Singapore

Contents

Introduction	4	Chatsworth House	42
The Goyt Valley and Edale	6	Dovedale	44
Snake Pass and Glossop	8	Tissington	46
Walking the Peak	10	Ashbourne	48
Castleton	12	Lakeland Derbyshire	50
Winnats Pass	14	Wirksworth	52
Stanage Edge and Hathersage	16	Cromford	54
Buxton	18	Matlock	56
Monsal Dale and Millers Dale	20	Ashover	58
Well-dressing	22	Crich	60
Eyam	24	Hardwick Hall	62
'Lover's Leap', Stoney Middleton	26	Belper	64
Baslow and Baslow Edge	28	Sudbury Hall and Doveridge Church	66
Chesterfield	30	Repton	68
Revolution House, Whittington	32	Swarkeston Bridge and Shardlow Marina	70
Bolsover Castle	34	Melbourne Hall	72
Lathkill Dale and Conksbury Bridge	36	Calke Abbey	74
Haddon Hall	38	Derby	76
Bakewell	40	Kedleston Hall	78

INTRODUCTION

Derbyshire is several counties in one, a 'Why go anywhere else?' sort of place, such is its variety. True, it lacks sea and sand, but no county can have *everything*. Travel from Swarkeston, where the land is so low-lying that it is crossed by a causeway, to the lofty wilderness of Kinder Scout; go from the dales of the Peak District to the coal-and-iron territory around Ripley and Alfreton. Whichever way you turn, it is like entering another country.

There is pastoral Derbyshire – the billowing patchwork quilt of fields spread before you near Cross o' the Hands and Idridgehay. There is 'roof of England' Derbyshire around Buxton. There is ribbon-development Derbyshire where the county nudges Nottinghamshire. There is the Derbyshire of gorges, around Matlock.

And there is 'backwoods' Derbyshire, which I first encountered in the 1950s. I had gone to attend a parish meeting one evening, at which it was confirmed that a village was to be drowned, submerged by Staunton Harold Reservoir. It was a far from joyous occasion, and at the meeting's conclusion both I and the clerk to the rural district council needed a drink.

We drove to a nearby pub which was also a smallholding. It was about 9 pm and the place was in darkness. The council clerk hammered on the door, and eventually we heard the patter of tiny feet. The door opened to reveal a pretty, fair-haired little girl in a nightgown holding a candle. She could not have been more than seven or eight. The clerk did not seem surprised or at all put out. I fancied he had been here before.

He hoisted the child on to the bar, from which she lit a mantle above her, and she then proceeded to serve us. I couldn't imagine how many laws were being broken, yet the scene had a touching innocence.

Paying for our beer, we drank it quickly enough not to keep the barmaid up too late. Then, wishing her good night, we departed. I had witnessed a little bit of Derbyshire history, for that hamlet is now under many feet of water.

But then, just about everywhere you look there are echoes of the past, together with evidence of history in the making. There are once-inhabited caves near Creswell, medieval fortified manors like Fenny Bentley Hall...and there is a £700 million car plant of the 1990s, the Toyota factory near Derby. Each item of the county's history mentioned in the following pages can be matched by yet another. Spare a thought, for instance, for the Newhaven Inn on the road from Buxton to Ashbourne. At the time of writing it stands forlorn and empty...and small wonder, you may think: fancy putting such a large establishment in the middle of nowhere. But it was built in 1795 to meet a need. It stood at the junction of turnpike roads, where coaches connected. It was the 'motorway services' of its day, with overnight guests including George IV, and stabling for 100 horses.

Another 'new' road has long intrigued visitors because of its Italianate name: the Via Gellia, so-called because it was built through its valley by the Gell family to enable lead from their mines to be transported to the Cromford Canal. That was in the late 18th century. In the more recent past, you could enjoy what was claimed to be the longest trolleybus ride in England, all 14 miles from Ripley to Nottingham. Settling in your seat, you could reflect on your trolleybus's precursors, the trams on that route celebrated in D.H. Lawrence's story, 'Tickets Please'.

Many another literary link is noted elsewhere in these pages, and Derbyshire has more: the Sitwells of Renishaw Hall; Richmal Crompton as a schoolgirl and teacher in Darley Dale; Evelyn Waugh as a guest in Edensor; John Osborne as a Derby Playhouse actor...

Did I hear someone say, 'And don't forget that the Duchess of Devonshire is Nancy Mitford's sister'? I haven't. Nor have I forgotten that D.H. Lawrence had a sister in Ripley, where a garage mechanic had been T.E. Lawrence's driver. But we could go on like this for ever.

Similarly, a tour of the stately homes here lasts somewhat longer than would be the case in most other counties. Derbyshire's embarrassment of riches in this respect is reflected in the pages which follow, where the amount of information is necessarily limited. So let me add a couple of items that you may not find in the guide books.

What's it like, working at Chatsworth? It can't be bad, because the last three head-gardeners have each been in Chatsworth's service for more than half-a-century. And what was it like to be lord of all you surveyed at Kedleston in the late 1940s? Hard-up. The then Lord Scarsdale serviced his own car, but at least he had beautiful surroundings in which to do it.

Many a visitor, enjoying the scenery on a balmy day, must think that Derbyshire is a good place to live, and they're right. But you have to be prepared for all seasons. In the exceptional winter of 1947, my wife's family were cut off by snow for six-and-a-half weeks. When my father-in-law set out to walk eight miles there-and-back to fetch hay for his beasts, he was able to find the way only by following the telephone wires which marked out the line of the road. But the views were marvellous....

William Amos
August 1995

The Goyt Valley and Edale

It was with a wry smile, some 30 years ago, that I read a guidebook's description of the road to Goyt's Bridge, near Buxton: 'The conditions prevent speeding, and the walker can feel safe'. The author was presumably unaware that this was used as a practice-run by rally drivers in search of snow and ice. More recently, the Peak Park Planning Board has restricted

vehicular access, but that is the least of the changes experienced by this valley.

It has become host to two reservoirs supplying Stockport and has seen the creation and demise of Errwood Hall, built in 1830 but abandoned when much of its land was submerged by the reservoir which bears its name and which has left little more than a fine display of rhododendrons as a reminder that someone once lived here. Similarly, the hamlet of Goyt's Bridge is no more. Yet the valley, noted for the variety of its vegetation, remains popular with ramblers.

If there is one place that is known by almost every walker, however, it is the village of Edale, a few miles to the north. It is here that the Pennine Way starts – or finishes, depending on which way you are going. And it is from here, surrounded by the looming terrain of Mam Tor, Crowden Head, Grindslow Knoll, Back Tor and The Nab, that numerous footpaths invite exploration of the Vale of Edale or ascent to the loftiest place in the county, the boggy plateau of Kinder Scout.

Should you wonder at the tautology of the Vale of Edale, here's the explanation. As the hamlet of Grindsbrook Booth expanded, encompassing a railway station, church and pub – the Old Nag's Head Inn (*inset*), dating from 1577 – it became Edale, taking the name of its valley. That meant there were now two Edales, so to avoid confusion the dale was given its vale prefix.

This may not justify the repetitiousness of the Vale of Edale, but it's certainly easier to say 'See you in Edale' than 'See you in Grindsbrook Booth' . . .

Snake Pass and Glossop

You might assume that Snake Pass owes its name to the way it snakes through the hills. Not so. It derives its title from the Snake Inn, at its eastern foot. And the pub, in turn, takes its name from the serpent that is the motif of the Cavendish family crest.

Come winter, the pass is usually among the first roads in Derbyshire to be blocked by snow, winding as it does through an elevated wilderness. It climbs to 1,680 ft above sea level as it traverses Featherbed Moss, before its descent to industrial Glossop (*inset*), a former cotton town encircled by looming moorland.

Thomas Telford was the 18th century builder of this highway which links Sheffield with Manchester, and travelling it by stage-coach must have been quite an experience. I still remember my first drive up the Snake, in foul weather, more than 30 years ago. I stopped by an AA box on Featherbed Moss, and as hail lashed my windows and wind rocked my car, I looked out on some of the least hospitable terrain I've ever encountered. Anyone who came here voluntarily in such weather, I reflected, must be a raving masochist. Years later, I was to be reminded of the scenery . . . in the Falklands.

I noticed that although few cars were on the road, there was no shortage of goods traffic. Perhaps some of those vehicles would pause at the Snake Inn, I thought, helping to make up the business lost by the pub when Sheffield was linked with Manchester by rail, via the Woodhead Tunnel, in the 1880s.

The Snake Inn had been built in 1821 to cater for those travelling the pass. Then, in the age of steam, much of the hostelry's custom evaporated. A long, lean period followed, until cars began to arrive and people rediscovered their feet; accounts of their walks noted how they welcomed the sight of the Snake Inn as they approached from the aptly-named Bleaklow Moor or Grim Seal Edge.

Walking the Peak

For hill-walkers, the Peak District of Derbyshire is more than a mecca. It is also a memory: of 24 April 1932, when 400 ramblers from Manchester trooped from Hayfield to William Clough, and then began scrambling up the slopes of Kinder Scout. What happened next made headlines, for that outing became the most dramatic mass trespass in a campaign by ramblers to secure public access to mountains and moorland.

The walkers soon found themselves confronted by gamekeepers. Scuffles ensued, and the keepers' sticks were torn from their hands. Some were forced to the ground, one of them rolling down the mountainside but suffering no more than a severe shaking.

Pressing on towards Ashop Head, the ramblers were then joined by a contingent from Sheffield, but on their

return to Hayfield they found a cordon of police blocking the road. Gamekeepers identified the walkers' leaders, and six were arrested.

Thirty years later, the writer Crichton Porteous noted that the plateau of Kinder Scout offers 'only bleakness under the sky, and to remember how close are the cotton, wool and steel towns to west and east is an effort'. Precisely. That, for the millworkers, was one of Kinder Scout's attractions.

The public's wish to stretch its legs on terrain exclusively the province of gamekeepers and grouse was recognised; access was granted, except at times of grouse-shooting, and Kinder Scout later became National Trust property...like Mam Tor (*opposite*) nearby, another walkers' favourite and otherwise known as 'The Shivering Mountain' due to its ever-shifting shale. The hill seems always to have had the shivers – in 1697, Celia Fiennes likened it to 'a great Hayricke thats cut down one halfe' and noted that 'the sand keeps trickling down all wayes'. The mystery is that Mam Tor, despite all that crumbling, never appears to get much smaller. So if the Iron Age settlers who built a fort on top had any anxiety about subsidence, they needn't have worried.

Although Kinder Scout rises to 2,000 ft, it is from Mam Tor's 1,700 ft summit that better views are enjoyed – of the Hope Valley and the Vale of Edale, with Kinder Scout looming beyond. And the footpath from Mam Tor to Lose Hill is acknowledged to be among the best ridge-walks in the Peak District.

THE MASS TRESPASS ONTO KINDER SCOUT STARTED FROM THIS QUARRY 24TH APRIL 1932

Castleton

Were one to compile a list of the Seven Wonders of Derbyshire, it would surely begin with the spectacular caverns at Castleton. Four separate complexes await the visitor: the Blue John, Speedwell, Peak and Treak Cliff Caverns.

Between them, they present a dazzling display of stalactites and stalagmites; Blue John, a translucent fluorspar peculiar to this area and mined since Roman times; an underground canal; fossils, and a rope-walk dating from the 15th century.

But as its name indicates, Castleton has another claim to attention. It is overlooked by the substantial remains of Peveril Castle – the county's only castle of significance, in the view of Sir Nikolaus Pevsner. This was built in the 11th century by William Peveril. No, he's not the hero of Sir Walter Scott's *Peveril of the Peak*, which is set in the 17th century, his Peveril being one of William's descendants.

Scott never went to the Isle of Man, where much of the novel's action takes place, and I doubt if he went to Castleton either. He describes the castle as a Gothic fortress – which it wasn't – and says it was built in a fashion suggesting it had been created for the sole purpose of puzzling posterity.

But you can see why Peveril chose the site. Such is the terrain that on three sides the castle is inaccessible, so its defenders had only one approach to worry about.

It is said that history was made here during the reign of Henry II in the 12th century, when England's king received the homage of the Scottish sovereign at Peveril Castle.

It is another monarch, however, whom Castleton chooses to commemorate on 29th May each year with Garland Day, which celebrates the restoration of Charles II in 1660. Accompanied by Castleton's band, a 'king' and his consort on horseback and in period costume lead a procession through the village to the market-place, where the maypole is decorated and Castleton's schoolgirls give a display of country dancing. The garland – a weighty affair adorning the king's shoulders – is then hoisted to decorate a pinnacle on the church tower.

Winnats Pass

Pronounced 'Winniates' by locals, Winnats means 'wind gates' – indicating that this pass near Castleton can be a blustery spot.

Where water must once have flowed, a road now winds through this mile-long gorge which is believed to have been used by animals as a migratory route, bison heading inland in summer and deer making for valleys near the coast in autumn and winter. The bones of wolves, bears, bison and reindeer have been found at Windy Knoll, at the head of the pass.

Wolves, however, were not the only predators. In 1748 a Scots couple eloped to marry at the chapel of Peak Forest, near Chapel-en-le-Frith, which at that time was a Derbyshire 'Gretna Green'. In Winnats Pass they were waylaid, robbed and murdered by four lead miners who had seen them break their journey at a Stoney Middleton inn and had ascertained their destination.

Although the couple's horses were found a few days later, there was no sign of the lovers . . . until years later, a shaft was being sunk in the pass, and a sack containing two skeletons was discovered.

More years elapsed, and then the death-bed confession of one of the miners revealed how the couple had been hacked to death for their money, amounting to about £200.

Stanage Edge and Hathersage

Where better to appreciate the full weight of 'a millstone round your neck' than Derbyshire? The county has them in profusion. Millstone grit composes the north of the Peak District, where producing millstones became an industry. Then the demand decreased and manufacturers were left with a surplus which has become part of the scenery at such millstone escarpments near Hathersage as Stanage Edge, on the Yorkshire border, and Millstone Edge, which provides not only the spectacle of millstones galore but also what is known as 'The Surprise', a panoramic view embracing the Derwent, Mam Tor, Kinder Scout, the Hope Valley and much else besides.

Hathersage (*inset*) began manufacturing knitting needles in the 16th century and also produced umbrella frames, but it is better known for other attributes. A grave about 11 ft long in the parish churchyard is reputed to be that of Little John, Robin Hood's companion, who is said to have been born in Hathersage. Tradition has it that he worked here as a nail-maker before he fought in Simon de Montfort's rebel army at Evesham in 1265, subsequently becoming an outlaw in Sherwood Forest.

The village is also the Morton of *Jane Eyre*, Charlotte Brontë taking the name of Hathersage's Eyre family for her heroine. The author stayed at the vicarage in 1845 with her friend Ellen Nussey, the vicar's sister, and North Lees Hall, Moorseats and Brookfield Manor have been identified with locations in the novel. The Revd St John Rivers is believed to have been based on the vicar of Hathersage, who proposed unsuccessfully to Charlotte Brontë, just as Rivers seeks the hand of Jane Eyre but is rejected. The author declared herself unable to accept the Revd Henry Nussey because she did not feel 'that intense attachment which would make me willingly die for him'.

Buxton

Noting in 1780 that Bath was booming, thanks to its spa waters, the fifth Duke of Devonshire decided that what Bath was for the south, Buxton could become for the north. The Romans who had savoured the mineral springs of Bath had also enjoyed the waters of Buxton, and the popularity of the Derbyshire town's springs had endured through the Middle Ages and into the Elizabethan era.

Taking Bath as his model, the Duke set about developing Buxton as a spa. A decade earlier, Bath had built its handsome Royal Crescent. The Duke therefore commissioned the York architect John Carr to create one for Buxton.

Completed in 1784, the outcome (*inset*) is one of Britain's architectural gems. But just as Buxton is a Bath in miniature, so is its Crescent smaller than its Bath predecessor, although arguably more elegant, recently receiving a £1 million grant from English Heritage.

Sadly Buxton did not persevere with its architectural renaissance, and cannot be compared to such spas as Bath, Cheltenham, Leamington or Harrogate, although the Victorians endowed it with the beguiling 23-acre Pavilion Gardens – pictured here – and 1905 saw the opening of the Opera House designed by the theatre-architect Frank Matcham.

Buxton's Devonshire Royal Hospital was formerly stables modelled on the Lipizaner establishment of the Spanish Riding School. In 1880 the building acquired what was then the largest dome in Britain, covering an open courtyard originally used for exercising horses.

After the vogue for 'taking the waters' faded, in the 1970s Buxton found a new attraction in music. In 1993 the annual Buxton International Festival of Music and the Arts attracted 25,000 visitors, who spent more than £750,000. Another innovation is the world's first micrarium, a see-for-yourself centre for the observation of nature through microscopes.

A somewhat different nature display is provided by Buxton's surrounding countryside, for when you travel from one side of the town to the other, the landscape changes. To the immediate west is bleak moorland where in 1947 snow still lay in June, with the carcasses of sheep which had died in the drifts.

Buxton, although in a valley, is more than a thousand feet above sea level. To the south, the terrain is pastoral . . . but elevated enough to remind you that it is not unusual to be cut off here by blizzards.

Monsal Dale and Millers Dale

John Ruskin was appalled. 'There was a rocky valley between Buxton and Bakewell, once upon a time, divine as the Vale of Tempe,' he wrote. 'You might have seen the gods there morning and evening – Apollo and all the sweet Muses of the light, walking in fair procession on the lawns, and to and fro among the pinnacles of its crags... but you enterprised a railroad through the valley – you blasted its rocks away, heaped thousands of tons of shale into its lovely stream. The valley is gone, and the gods with it, and now every fool in Buxton can be in Bakewell in half an hour, and every fool in Bakewell at Buxton.'

In the 1860s, a railway viaduct had been built across Monsal Dale. A handsome structure, as viaducts go, but in Ruskin's eyes it desecrated the landscape; and were a new motorway bridge to span some favourite beauty spot today, our reaction would doubtless be the same.

But we who have never seen Monsal Dale (*inset*) without its viaduct find it difficult to picture the valley without it. Far from desecrating the scene, it seems to enhance it, providing a focal point much favoured by photographers. It has become as much a part of Monsal Dale as Ruskin's 'lawns' and crags, and when the railway ceased to operate in the late 1960s and there was talk of demolishing the viaduct, there was an outcry to preserve it. So now it is part of a trail for ramblers and cyclists, its steam train heyday a happy memory for 'fools' like me who enjoyed what was surely one of the most beautiful railway routes anywhere.

Millers Dale (*opposite*), through which the Wye flows into Monsal Dale, takes its name from the corn-milling carried out there for centuries. Its Litton cotton mill, however, became notorious for its exploitation of child-labour – boys were brought from London as 'parish apprentices', one of them becoming a putative prototype for Dickens's Oliver Twist.

This was Robert Blincoe who in 1833 told a House of Commons inquiry into child labour of the privation he experienced as a workhouse child employed at Litton Mill.

Well-dressing

This is pre-eminently a Derbyshire craft. Nowhere else is it so widespread or practised so assiduously. Believed to date from pagan times, it originated as an expression of gratitude for the provision of water, and supplication for a continued supply.

Today it often celebrates communities' appreciation of other benefits. It is perhaps best displayed at Tissington, near Ashbourne, where six wells are dressed for Ascension Day. Nobody knows just how long Tissington has dressed its wells; the custom can be traced back to the mid 18th century with certainty, and the 17th century with probability – when traditionally the hamlet's springs kept flowing throughout the acute drought of 1615.

If you fancy dressing a well, here's how to set about it. First, acquire a stout, wooden screen which must be thoroughly soaked. Your board must also be liberally studded with nails, protruding about a quarter of an inch. These are required to key your clay which, 'puddled' with salt and water, will cover one side of your screen to a depth of up to an inch.

Having drawn your design on a large piece of paper, place it on the clay and prick out the lines of your picture. Then remove the paper, and make your prick-marks in the clay more apparent by replacing them with berries or small cones. Finally, fill in your design by pressing on to the clay the flower-petals and other foliage of your choice, remembering to work from the bottom to the top, ensuring that each petal is overlapped by the one above it, so that rainwater is not collected.

The well-dressings pictured here are Marston Montgomery's aerial view of itself, and *(inset)* Litton's celebration of The Year of the Family.

Eyam

Five miles from Bakewell, Eyam today presents a picture of serenity, its mellow 17th century hall overlooking the green. But in 1665 the village became a scene of unimaginable horror. Its story is one of stoicism in the face of overwhelming adversity, of humbling self-sacrifice, and of a clergyman who, put to the most agonising of tests, was not found wanting.

In September that year a bolt of cloth arrived in Eyam for a tailor. It had come from London, then ravaged by bubonic plague, and the germs that accompanied the cloth soon killed the tailor and infected others in the village. Eyam's problem was how to stop the plague spreading; the squire and his family fled, so someone else had to take the lead. The Revd William Mompesson, rector of Eyam, stepped forward.

To confine the outbreak to the village, he persuaded his parishioners to stay. Nobody was to leave, and no one must enter. It was arranged for supplies to be left at a safe distance from the village. Not everybody heeded the rector's call, but some 350 parishioners complied. According to one account, all but 33 succumbed to the plague. Mompesson's wife was among them.

'My ears never heard such doleful lamentations. My nose never smelt such noisome smells, and my eyes never beheld such ghastly spectacles', the rector recorded. In a single week, one woman buried her husband and six of her seven children.

The dwelling where the tailor lodged, now called Plague Cottage, remains to this day, as does the rock from which the rector preached when he felt that assembling his congregation in church might lead to the epidemic becoming even more virulent. Also outside the village is what is now known as Mompesson's Well, in which payment was left for food delivered, the coins being washed in vinegar and water in the belief that this would act as a disinfectant. And on a hillside are the graves of plague victims (*inset*), buried there after the churchyard was closed during the outbreak.

Mompesson's chair is preserved in the church, and each year on the last Sunday in August the congregation goes to the rock, his other place of worship, where tribute is paid to those who perished in 1665-66 and to the few who survived.

'Lover's Leap', Stoney Middleton

The story of the pioneer parachutist, told in the picture on this page, is not the only Stoney Middleton curiosity. One squire of the village thought so highly of the black pigs he bred that he assumed his friends must hold them in the same esteem. He would roll up in his carriage, accompanied by one of his pigs . . . but it would not be with him on his return journey. He was delivering it as a present.

He lived at Stoney Middleton Hall, which was also the home of his father, the first Lord Denman, who defended Queen Caroline when George IV tried unsuccessfully to divorce her, and who subsequently became Lord Chief Justice.

The parish church was built by Joan Padley in thanksgiving for the safe return of her husband from Agincourt, but only the tower of that structure remains. The rest of the church was replaced in 1759, with what is still a novelty: an octagonal nave.

At one time, many of the village's cottagers were employed in their homes as out-workers, producing boots and shoes for a local factory. They were assured of a steady demand: in a place where streets were so steep, walking was the most practical way of getting around, as a village dignitary explained when he was asked why he did not keep a coach. Stoney Middleton, he said, stood on end.

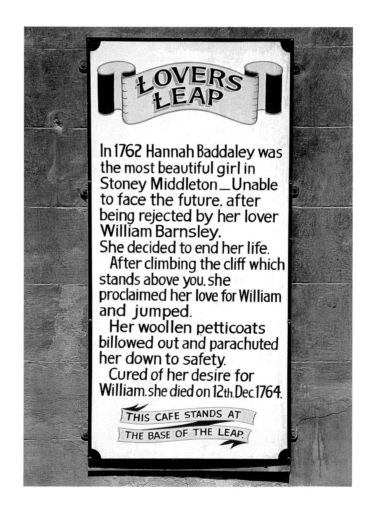

LOVERS LEAP

In 1762 Hannah Baddaley was the most beautiful girl in Stoney Middleton — Unable to face the future, after being rejected by her lover William Barnsley. She decided to end her life.

After climbing the cliff which stands above you, she proclaimed her love for William and jumped.

Her woollen petticoats billowed out and parachuted her down to safety.

Cured of her desire for William, she died on 12th. Dec. 1764.

THIS CAFE STANDS AT THE BASE OF THE LEAP.

Baslow and Baslow Edge

Connoisseurs of toll-houses say that England's smallest is at Baslow, near Chatsworth. As its doorway is only three-and-a-half feet high, I believe them. The minuscule building stands at the village end of a picturesque, triple-arched packhorse bridge, but Baslow's principal attraction is the beautiful setting of its parish church, on the banks of the Derwent.

One face of the church clock has VICTORIA 1897 instead of numerals, so it's no surprise to find a Victorian ambience within, for the building has been much restored. The tower, however, dates from the 13th century, and the church's artefacts include the remains of a Saxon cross and a whip for driving out dogs.

The Peak District is not an area where you would expect to find thatched cottages, but (*inset*) Baslow has them, by its Goose Green. It's the kind of place that wins best-kept village contests without even trying.

The escarpment of Baslow Edge, pictured opposite from Curbar Edge, provides a good view of the Derwent valley and Chatsworth Park, and neighbouring Gardom's Edge is noted for curious patterns cut in its rock. Nobody knows their meaning.

Chesterfield

This town owes its celebrated landmark of a twisted church spire to a botched job. There are those who will tell you that lightning was responsible. Don't believe them. The accepted explanation for this Chesterfield curiosity is that unseasoned timber was used in the spire's construction. Consequently, the wood warped.

One theory has it that green timber was used because the spire was built following a plague, which caused a shortage of skilled craftsmen. The spire's carpenters didn't realise that seasoned wood was required, and when the sun warmed the heavy lead cladding, the timber distorted.

Ironically, had the job been done properly, Chesterfield would be less well known than it is today, as a Derbyshire 'Pisa' . . . for the spire also leans: to the south, at an angle which has become increasingly pronounced over the years.

It was in this church that the rebellious sixth Earl of Derby took refuge in 1266 after Royalists routed his private army at Chesterfield. He was discovered concealed among sacks of wool, and punished for his escapade by being deprived of most of his property. Although parts of this church of Our Lady and All Saints date from that time, the building is primarily of 14th century construction, with 18th century additions.

Derbyshire's largest town – since Derby became a city – Chesterfield is an industrial centre, with a long history. The Romans built a fort here, and the 16th-century timber-framed Royal Oak Inn is a replacement

for premises used by the Knights Templar during the Crusades.

It was in 1204 that King John granted Chesterfield the right to hold markets, but although the royal charter was doubtless appreciated its recipients had already been holding markets for at least four decades. Now there are three a week, and Chesterfield claims to have England's largest regular open market.

For railway buffs, however, the significance of Chesterfield is that it was here that George Stephenson spent his last years. The town became his base during his construction of the North Midland line from Derby to Leeds, and he is buried at Chesterfield's Holy Trinity church.

Revolution House, Whittington

Some say that the four noblemen were driven by a storm to seek shelter at Whittington's Cock and Pynot Inn. Others claim that they left a hunt on Whittington moor, slipping away to make for the inn when the pack was in full cry. But there is no dispute about what brought them together. They were plotting the overthrow of their king.

It was June 1688, and James II had turned out to be a zealous Catholic, removing Protestants from their posts to replace them with Catholics and dissolving Parliament in order to reconstitute it with a Catholic majority.

The Earl of Devonshire wanted to see the back of him. So did the Earl of Danby, Baron Delamere and the Earl of Holderness's heir. They all wished to see James's Protestant son-in-law, Prince William of Orange, on the English throne.

At the Cock and Pynot – since you ask, a pynot's a magpie – the four met in what later became known as 'The Plotting Parlour'. The Earl of Devonshire took the chair, and it was agreed that while he raised an army in the Midlands, Danby was to do the same in the North, Delamere mustering forces in Cheshire. There had already been two unsuccessful rebellions, the last put down with a savagery that had shocked the nation. This time the uprising would be better organised, and more widespread.

Devonshire and Danby were among seven prominent men who put their coded signatures to a letter to Prince William urging him to raise an army and sail for England to restore liberty. At the end of the month, the letter was on its way to Holland in the hands of Admiral Arthur Herbert, disguised as an ordinary seaman.

William of Orange was further encouraged by hearing that James could not rely on the support of his 30,000-strong army. Another spur to action was the birth in June of James's son: this meant that the king's Protestant daughter Mary and her husband, the Dutch ruler, could no longer hope to attain the English throne through natural succession.

On 5th November, William and his army landed at Torbay, but his troops were hardly needed. He was welcomed all the way to London. James fled, and was caught and imprisoned under a guard lax enough for him to escape and flee to France, where he arrived on Christmas Day, 1688.

William and Mary were duly crowned – James was considered to have abdicated by throwing his seal of office into the Thames. The Earl of Devonshire was elevated to duke, and others whose services were recognised included the courier admiral, who became the Earl of Torrington.

Three hundred years after the conspirators met in Whittington, Prince Charles flew there to join the present Duke of Devonshire and descendants of the other plotters in an anniversary celebration. But the Cock and Pynot had changed since 1688. No longer an inn, its 'Plotting Parlour' gone, it has become Revolution House, its interior a museum.

Bolsover Castle

Even today, blowing £15,000 on an evening's entertainment might be considered extravagant. In 1634 it must have been positively staggering. But then, the principal guests were Charles I and his queen, and Ben Jonson had written a masque, *Love's Welcome at Bolsover*, specially for the occasion. Bolsover Castle was the location, and the host footing the bill was the Earl of Newcastle, the monarch's former tutor. Earlier at Welbeck Abbey, his other home, he had spent £20,000 entertaining James I.

Newcastle later became one of Charles's defeated generals, retiring abroad after the Royalist rout at Marston Moor. He was also a grandson of Bess of Hardwick, which helps to explain the grandiose nature of Bolsover Castle. Like his father, he inherited Bess's building mania.

William the Conqueror gave Bolsover to his bailiff, William Peveril, who is believed to have built a keep where Bolsover Castle stands today. In 1613, Bess's son, Sir Charles Cavendish, leased the site and – apparently obsessed by Arthurian legend – began his battlements-and-turrets essay of make-believe in masonry. By the time of his death four years later, much of the nucleus of Bolsover Castle was complete, but it wasn't enough for his son.

Sir William – subsequently Earl and then Duke of Newcastle – started by building a horse-training hall (*inset*) nearby, later linking this to the castle-proper with a range of buildings which included a gallery. Although much of his creation is now ruinous, the shell endures on its ridge as a dramatic spectacle. His grandmother would have been proud of him.

Lathkill Dale and Conksbury Bridge

Those in search of peace find it in this quiet dale, which having no road along its length is free from traffic. It is noted for its Lake District erratics, rocks carried down by Ice Age glaciers; for its limestone cliffs and, by botanists, as a rare Peak District home of blue Jacob's ladder. For industrial archaeologists there are lead mining relics – the Lathkill Dale Mining Company operated until 1842.

The dale is also known for the vivid hues of its waters, said by the 17th century angling writer Charles Cotton to be the purest and most translucent he had ever seen. But they have a habit of drying up in the Lathkill's upper reaches, and in hot weather are best observed in pools below nearby Over Haddon.

This was the home of Martha Taylor, who seems to have been a pioneer anorexic. An invalid from childhood, she is remembered for subsisting for a year when she was about 18 on a diet consisting of no more than raisin-juice, prune-syrup and the occasional drop of sugar and water. After this regimen, she endured for a further 17 years, dying in 1684.

Once upon a time there was presumably a hamlet called Conksbury. Now the name seems to be preserved only in the dale's Conksbury Bridge (*inset*), its low arches testimony to the local limestone's role in absorbing much of the surface water: whoever built this squat span was apparently confident that it was high enough to cope with the river, even in spate.

Haddon Hall

Of all the stately homes in Derbyshire, Haddon Hall, I suspect, is the one where most visitors would like to live. It has none of the grandeur of Chatsworth, none of the pomp of Hardwick Hall. It is a home, rather than a showplace.

For 200 years, however, it was unoccupied. And it is thanks to that long spell of virtual abandonment that it owes its escape from periodic alteration – the building of extensions, the replacement of a wing here, a staircase there – which over the centuries has been the experience of many another stately home. This is not to say that Haddon Hall has remained unchanged since the 12th century; only that alterations have been modest compared, for instance, with the development of Chatsworth. And those improvements have been charmingly haphazard. It is as if Haddon Hall has somehow grown over the centuries of its own accord, without the dubious benefit of architects.

Most of the developments which took place were prompted by the changing practical needs of the day, rather than by the foibles of fashion. Thus, when fortification was no longer necessary, Haddon Hall acquired a new entrance. Significant alterations ceased in the 17th century, and when you stand in the building's banqueting hall you see nothing – the renewed roof excepted – that is not much as it was in 1600, although the room itself is at least 200 years older.

During its years of desertion, Haddon Hall was not surprisingly described as gloomy and melancholy. For four centuries it had been owned by the Vernon family. In 1567 John Manners, brother of the second Earl of Rutland, married Dorothy Vernon and Haddon subsequently became the Rutlands' principal home, prior to their inheritance of Belvoir Castle. Then, it seems, they found themselves with one stately home too many, and an empty Haddon was all but forgotten.

Vacant though it was for two centuries, however, it remained structurally sound. Rescue from further neglect came in 1912, when two decades of sensitive restoration were initiated by the ninth Duke of Rutland.

At last, Haddon was appreciated again, its romantic 17th century gardens replanted with roses: the sort of place Dornford Yates must have had in mind, I fancy, when he created 'White Ladies', the ancestral home of the Pleydells in the 'Berry' stories. When the Pleydells finally departed they gave their home to the nation, rather than make a fortune selling it to be rebuilt in America. After all, 'White Ladies' had belonged to England for so long…just as Haddon Hall has belonged to the present Duke of Rutland and his ancestors since 1153.

Bakewell

The day something went wrong in the kitchen something went right for Bakewell. Preparing a pudding at the town's Rutland Arms Hotel, the cook inadvertently put the egg mixture on to the jam instead of into the pastry. One fancies that the cook's employer – a sister-in-law of Sir Joseph Paxton – was not best pleased. But the pudding didn't taste bad. In fact, it was uncommonly good. Nobody had savoured anything quite like it, and it wasn't long before Bakewell became a household name, Mrs Beeton detailing how to make two varieties of Bakewell pudding – 'very rich' and 'plainer'.

The cook's mistake put the town on the culinary map, and it was decided to keep secret precisely what had gone into the original pudding. Nowadays most of us know the confection as Bakewell tart, although the town's Bakewell pudding shops retain the old description, two of them claiming to use the original recipe.

In contrast to the happy accident in the kitchen, everything else in Bakewell seems to have been planned. King Alfred's son, Edward, is believed to have sited a fort here to repel Danish invaders; the town was in 1254 granted a charter to hold markets, which flourish to this day – the cattle market is one of the busiest in the county; in the 18th century Richard Arkwright extended his cotton-spinning empire by building a mill in Bakewell, where he also acquired a mistress; Bakewell Show, a premier annual agricultural event in the county, was instituted in 1843; and Bakewell is now the headquarters of the Peak Park Planning Board.

The warm springs enjoyed by the Romans at Bakewell – the town's name derives from the Saxon *bad-quell*, 'bath-well' – were not of the quality of those of Buxton, however, and efforts to turn the place into a spa were unsuccessful, although the town's visitors included Jane Austen, in whose *Pride and Prejudice* Bakewell becomes Lambton and Chatsworth appears as Pemberley. The Duke of Rutland's Bath House is now occupied by the British Legion.

But if the Duke whose spa dream failed to materialise were to see Bakewell today, he would marvel at the number of visitors the town now attracts both as a base for touring the Peak District and as simply a pleasant place to be. Awaiting those visitors is a graceful bridge, almost 700 years old; a parish church of even greater antiquity; and the town's elegant 17th, 18th and early 19th century buildings . . . among them the Rutland Arms Hotel of 1804, where that kitchen mishap has ensured that many have heard of Bakewell who have never been there.

Chatsworth House

On first seeing the opulence of this palatial building, which makes many another stately home seem a poor relation in comparison, my father said that he now knew why there had been a French revolution. But then, Chatsworth is no stranger to the threat of insurrection. Long before today's house took shape, Mary Queen of Scots spent five periods of captivity here in the 1570s and '80s. Even then, the house was an eye-opener, the Elizabethan creation of the first Earl of Devonshire's mother, Bess of Hardwick.

The Chatsworth House that attracts visitors today began to take shape in 1687. The old home was gradually demolished by the fourth Earl, soon after he became the first Duke of Devonshire in recognition of his role in easing the way of William of Orange to the throne.

It is to the first Duke that Chatsworth owes its most

impressive façade, the west front, and the superb woodcarving once popularly attributed to Grinling Gibbons, but now known to be primarily the work of a Derbyshire craftsman, Samuel Watson of Heanor, who also executed Chatsworth's elegant stone carving.

The first Duke's building activity ended with his death in 1707. Half a century later, the fourth Duke created the grandiose stables and the graceful bridge spanning the Derwent. He also landscaped the grounds, with the assistance of 'Capability' Brown. Between 1820 and 1842, the sixth Duke added the north wing and converted the long gallery into a library.

Departing visitors take away different memories, perhaps most notably the overwhelming splendour of the State Rooms and the spectacle of the grounds' Cascade, dating from 1694. My own abiding recollection is of something less dramatic. Standing proud of woods to the north-east of the house is Chatsworth's Hunting Tower. It looks like a folly, but doubtless once fulfilled a useful role as a look-out post. Unlike the present Chatsworth House, it was part of the scenery when Mary Queen of Scots paid her involuntary visits, and she must have been familiar with it, looking much as it does today.

Soon after her arrival at Chatsworth, a plot was hatched to free her. The conspirators met on the moors nearby, but one of them talked and they were imprisoned. Meanwhile, Mary is said to have strolled in the roof-garden of another of Chatsworth's surviving Elizabethan outbuildings, Queen Mary's Bower.

Dovedale

Some years ago, I had visitors who were going to Dovedale. On their return, I asked if they had enjoyed it. Yes, they replied, without any great enthusiasm. It transpired that they hadn't left the car park. Once there, they thought that was it. They'd seen Dovedale. 'You might as well say you've seen the "Mona Lisa",' I told them, 'when you've seen only the frame.'

They had touched only the fringe of this celebrated limestone gorge which is so dramatic, so romantic, so varied and so beautiful that it seems almost too good to be true. Perhaps it's just as well that there's only two miles of it: any more could give you visual indigestion.

Cars have long been mercifully kept at a distance, but the less energetic among our predecessors explored Dovedale on donkeys and on horseback. Byron ranked the gorge with the scenery of Greece and Switzerland; Samuel Johnson said that he who had seen Dovedale needn't trouble to visit the Highlands; Izaak Walton celebrated the Dove's fishing in *The Compleat Angler*; and Tennyson, heedless of what grammarians might say, described Dovedale as 'one of the most unique and delicious places in England'.

Such is the ever-changing scene awaiting walkers progressing through the gorge that it's as if it had been landscaped to beguile, with curious, water-sculpted rock formations like the Lion's Head and the arch on the approach to Reynard's Cave deftly placed as conversation pieces. Other landmarks include rocks known as the Twelve Apostles, the pinnacles of Ilam

Rock and Pickering Tor (*inset*), the twin caves called the Dove Holes (*opposite*) and the cone-shaped hill poetically named Thorpe Cloud.

Tissington

This is quite the last place where you would expect to find graffiti. But if it did appear, an appropriate message would be 'Autocracy Rules OK'. For Tissington owes its unspoilt charm not to planning regulations, but to the fact that it is an estate village, the domain of the FitzHerberts who have lived here for more than four centuries. Thus the hamlet has been spared inharmonious developments of the kind that blight many once-picturesque villages.

Approached from the Buxton-Ashbourne road via a lodge entrance and avenue, Tissington is an idyllic backwater save at summer weekends and during its celebrated well-dressing. Then it falls prey to its beauty, attracting countless visitors. Its dwellings are grouped and sited individually in a manner which seems gloriously unplanned – paradoxically, the best form of planning. So the village has the appearance of a happy accident, which is perhaps what the lords of the manor intended in the mid-19th century when much of the building took place, supplementing such earlier creations as a Georgian house, a Norman church and the Jacobean Tissington Hall.

The FitzHerberts' chaplain in the 1740s was Richard Graves, a close friend of Ralph Allen, the model for Squire Allworthy in Fielding's *Tom Jones*. Thirty years later, Graves became a best-selling novelist with *The Spritual Quixote*, in which his former Tissington employer appeared as Sir William Forester, 'a gentleman of fine sense, and, what is not always a consequence, of fine taste, not only in the polite arts, music, painting, architecture, and the like, but in life and manners. He had the art of making every company happy, and the greater art of making himself happy in every company'.

Samuel Johnson concurred. 'There is no sparkle, no brilliancy in FitzHerbert,' he said, 'but I never knew a man who was so generally acceptable. He made everybody quite easy, overpowered nobody by the superiority of his talents, made no man think worse of himself by being his rival, seemed always to listen, did not oblige you to hear much from him, and did not oppose what you said. Everybody liked him.'

Later FitzHerberts were to achieve eminence, one as the most distinguished diplomat of his day, another as the wife of George IV. But the self-effacing FitzHerbert, so warmly regarded by Johnson, is remembered for an exchange chronicled by Boswell.

A poet acquaintance was making a great show of anxiety over a son who was away at school, saying that the boy might be ill and declaring how much he wished to see him. To take his mind off this worry, the poet continued, he would write an elegy.

'Had you not better,' said FitzHerbert, 'take a post-chaise and go and see him?'

Ashbourne

Towns with literary associations tend to be beguiling: writers appreciate a nice place. Samuel Johnson often visited Ashbourne, staying at The Mansion opposite the 16th century Grammar School, with James Boswell at the Green Man Inn (*inset*); Elizabeth Gaskell stayed at Ashbourne Hall; at his Mayfield cottage two miles away, the poet Thomas Moore wrote 'Those Evening Bells', celebrating the peal of Ashbourne's St Oswald's, extolled by George Eliot as 'the finest mere parish church in the kingdom'; and here, as curate, W. Keble Martin – of *Concise British Flora* renown – met an Ashbourne girl who became his wife, having earlier proved her worth by holding his ankles to stop him falling into Bentley Brook in his flower-hunting.

Today you are more likely to meet antiques-hunters, for whom Ashbourne has shops lining Church Street,

arguably the county's most architecturally interesting thoroughfare, which I find impossible to walk without thinking of those who have passed this way before . . . Boswell hanging on to Johnson's every word, Keble Martin off to sketch knotted pearlwort on Ashbourne Green, and even Bonnie Prince Charlie, who spent a couple of nights in Ashbourne where he was proclaimed king.

And Penelope Boothby, whose death in 1791 at the age of six endowed St Oswald's with what must surely be one of the most touching monuments in any church, anywhere. Said to have moved Queen Caroline to tears, the child's white marble effigy is inscribed: 'She was in form and intellect most exquisite, The unfortunate Parents ventured their all on this frail Bark, And the wreck was total'. Never mind the stilted language of the time. You know they meant every word of it.

While Penelope sleeps on in St Oswald's, Ashbourne gets on with life. Shrove Tuesday and Ash Wednesday bring traffic to a halt as the town's Shrovetide foot-ballers take to the streets, in a no-holds-barred, shops boarded-up battle between those from north of Henmore Brook and those residing to the river's south. The custom has endured for centuries, but since 1928 – when the Prince of Wales was the celebrity who threw the ball into the throng to start the annual mayhem – it has been *Royal* Shrovetide Football. Despite Bonnie Prince Charlie's short-lived 'reign', Ashbourne takes its royals seriously.

Lakeland Derbyshire

Derbyshire is a county of reservoirs, and that at Carsington – pictured below – is the latest. Between Wirksworth and Ashbourne, it was opened in 1992, complete with visitor centre and water sports. One guide book describes it as 'controversial', but reservoirs always are until they become an accepted part of the scenery and the memory of what they have drowned has faded.

Derbyshire's Ladybower reservoir (*opposite*), completed in 1945, submerged the villages of Derwent and Ashopton, the ruins of which reappear at times of drought, but Ladybower is now regarded as a visual asset. It is the southernmost in a chain of reservoirs – 'one dam thing after another', said my father – and its Derwent Valley neighbours, Howden Dam (1912) and Derwent Dam (1916), were used by the RAF's 'Dambusters' in their experiments with the bouncing bomb devised by Dr Barnes Wallis, a native of Ripley.

Howden Dam is also the site of a memorial tablet commemorating Tip, a sheepdog who for 15 weeks stayed by the body of her master after he collapsed and died on a nearby moor. Tip's icy vigil began on 12th December 1953 and ended on 27th March 1954, when the emaciated collie was discovered still guarding her owner's corpse. She died just under a year later, and was buried where she and her master had been found.

Nobody knows how Tip managed to survive so long on the moor, and – for me – there's another local mystery. Drive from Ladybower to Howden and back again, and you will find that for parts of the journey you can free-wheel in both directions. I can't explain it. All I can tell you is that it happens.

Wirksworth

In Wirksworth in the 1840s there was one door which was perhaps best avoided. Behind it lived a Methodist lay-preacher, Elizabeth Evans, who in her prime 'could not rest without exhorting and remonstrating in season and out of season', according to her niece, the novelist George Eliot.

But it was this aunt who provided Eliot with the Hetty Sorrel episode in *Adam Bede*, based on Elizabeth Evans's account of accompanying to the gallows a young mother convicted of infanticide. The aunt's husband was the manager of a tape mill in Wirksworth, the 'Snowfield' of *Adam Bede*.

Given that setting, the novel naturally features lead-mining, for which the Wirksworth district was noted from Roman times. In the eighth century, Wirksworth supplied a lead coffin for a saint buried in Lincolnshire, and in the ninth century it was Wirksworth lead which repaired the roof of Christ Church, Canterbury. The town's Barmote Court, which still supervises lead-mining in the Low Peak, dates from around this time, although the mining of lead in the area has now all but ceased.

Known as 'Wassa' by those for whom 'Wirksworth' is too much of a mouthful, the town seems to wrap its arms around its parish church, giving the setting of St Mary's the ambience of a cathedral close. And once a year, the church is literally embraced by its parishioners, who join hands and surround their place of worship in the ceremony of 'clypping' – a tradition also practised in Tideswell.

But then, Wirksworth's church is an unusually fine one, as befits a parish which two centuries ago was the county's fourth largest town. Although St Mary's is primarily late 13th century, with considerable 19th century restoration, its foundation dates from 653 and the most dramatic evidence of its Anglo-Saxon origin was unearthed in 1820, with the discovery of the stone lid of a saint's coffin, profusely decorated with carvings chronicling scenes from the life of Christ.

Seven years after that ancient artefact came to light, Wirksworth had something else to celebrate: street taps. At last, the town had a municipal water supply. So it gave thanks with well-dressing, which has continued annually ever since 1827, Wirksworth dressing nine wells more than anywhere else in the county.

Cromford

It was here in 1771 that Sir Richard Arkwright laid the foundation of the next century's prosperity. His Cromford cotton mill was the first to be powered by water, establishing a system that was to be copied by mill-owners throughout the north of England and elsewhere, and pioneering mass-production. If any one man can be said to have fathered the Industrial Revolution, that man is Arkwright, who began his working life as a Bolton barber.

In Nottingham, he built a horse-driven mill, having been exiled from his native Lancashire by workers' machine-wrecking opposition to his inventions, which were seen as a threat to employment. His spinning-frame was to transform the textile industry and make his fortune.

Hampered by the inadequacies of horse-power, he looked to water as a solution, and to the Derwent and its tributaries at Cromford for the location of a mill the like of which the world had never seen. His Lancashire memories determined the fortress-like design of the factory he developed in partnership with Jedediah Strutt, and his employees revered and loved him: he built them cottages, a church and an inn, a model village in a beautiful valley.

He died – still speaking broad 'Lancashire', still semi-literate – before the church was completed, leaving the work to be finished by his son. How would he have fared in an age in which progress is regulated by exams? I think he would still have prospered through sheer native wit. As Sir Peter Ustinov has observed, those who reach the top tend to lack the qualifications that would detain them at the bottom.

Our two views show Cromford as seen from Black Rock.

Matlock

The warm springs at Matlock Bath began to attract attention in 1698, and the district's first therapeutic bath was built – with wood, lined with lead. A century and a half was to pass, however, before the spas of Matlock Bath and neighbouring Matlock Bank became fashionable.

Having benefited from the Matlock waters himself, the textile manufacturer John Smedley bought a house at Matlock Bank in about 1850, taking six patients. From this modest beginning, his establishment expanded to become a vast complex, and in 1867 Smedley's Hydropathic Hotel treated no fewer than 2,000, while other visitors patronised the numerous hydros opened by competitors who had followed Smedley's lead. The district had become 'The Metropolis of Hydropathy'.

This development came too late for Matlock to achieve the architectural appeal of such spas as Leamington or Cheltenham, but the Derbyshire resort enjoyed one advantage denied those rivals: a spectacular setting. Occupying a gorge through which the river Derwent flows between the towering High Tor and the even loftier Heights of Abraham, Matlock Bath in particular is like nowhere else in England.

Visitors including Byron, Ruskin, D.H. Lawrence and John Betjeman have found it captivating, but as the hydros' popularity began to wane, local entrepreneurs decided that the gorge's natural beauty wasn't enough. Other attractions were needed: Venetian nights with illuminated boats cruising the river, and a cable car for

the 750 ft ascent to the top of the Heights of Abraham, for a look at the view and a visit to caverns once mined for lead by the Romans. There is now also an aquarium, a model railway display, a museum of mining and an extensive pleasure ground with a variety of excitements for children.

Ashover

Had you been here in the late summer of 1925, you might have encountered a tall, gangling, blue-eyed man of 20 just down from Oxford. He had taken an unsalaried, short-term post as private tutor to the ten-year-old son of a widow living at Ashover Grange, and he was staying at the Ambervale Hotel which, world-wearily, he described as 'comic'. There, at the writing-table in the billiard-room, he applied himself to penning at least 500 words a day. This self-imposed discipline became a joke among the hotel staff and guests. He'd had little success as yet, but the daily routine was to endure throughout his life and the literary world was to hear more of him. His name was Graham Greene.

Another Ashover establishment, however, has a less beguiling story. During the Civil War, a number of Royalist soldiers descended on the Crispin Inn. They were drunk and the landlord refused to serve them, so they threw him out and helped themselves, drinking the pub dry. Then, on behalf of the king, they demanded £10 each from Ashover's rector and two parishioners, and on being asked to accept less they accused the reluctant donors of being Roundheads and threatened to burn down their homes. Eight miles from Chesterfield, Ashover was much afflicted by successive tides of Royalists and Parliamentarians. The rector became a victim again when Roundheads demanded £20 from him, saying they would take his cattle in lieu if he didn't pay. Then more Royalists arrived, 'like demons destroying all they came neare and left the poore to starve', the rector recorded. But the cleric's troubles had hardly begun. In 1646 the Roundheads returned, blowing up his home – Eastwood Hall – lest it fall into enemy hands, but singing a hymn before they went on to vandalise his 13th century church and burn the parish register: because it was in Latin, he said, they assumed it must be 'full of popery and treason'.

Happily, the church's notable Norman lead font and the fine 16th century alabaster tomb of Thomas Babington – credited with building the tower and spire – escaped damage. And as the inscriptions of 18th century tablets indicate, calmer times soon returned. One pays tribute to a parishioner whose 'superior performance on the bassoon endeared him to an extensive musical acquaintance'. Another notes the passing of a worshipper who 'became wonderful proficient in the gentler art of painting'.

In 1660 Ashover also became the last resting-place of Dorothy Mately, a foul-mouthed lead-washer at a local mine. Whenever she was accused of misdemeanours – which was often – she would say she wished the ground would open and swallow her up should she be guilty. When a workmate claimed she had stolen twopence from him, she repeated her habitual declaration of innocence . . . which was tempting fate in a mining area liable to sudden subsidence. The ground beneath her promptly opened and she disappeared. Her body was recovered, but not her life. Ironically, she was to achieve immortality, her example recorded as a warning to others in Bunyan's *The Life and Death of Mr Badman*.

This House probably dates from the Year 1410 when THOMAS BABINGTON of DETHICK and several men of ASHER returned from the BATTLE of AGINCOURT which was fought on ST CRISPIN'S DAY

In 1646 JOB WALL the Landlord of the INN withstood the Kings Troops in the doorway and told them that they should have no more drink in his house as they had had too much already. But they turned him out and set watch at the door till all the ale was drunk or wasted.

The above incident occurred during the period when the Troops of KING CHARLES I^t were opposing OLIVER CROMWELL'S ARMY

THE CRISPIN INN

Crich

This village is remarkable for two reasons. It has what at first sight appears to be a lighthouse marooned on a cliff in the middle of England. And it is the last place where you might expect to find a celebrated tramway museum.

The 'lighthouse', a beacon 950 ft above sea level, is Crich Stand (*inset*), war memorial of the Sherwood Foresters (Nottinghamshire and Derbyshire Regiment), whose depot was at Derby. Their proud history, bristling with battle honours, did not preserve them in our own time from amalgamation with the Worcestershire Regiment, a move which defied geography, logic and local sentiment – the Worcesters were not even fellow-members of the Midland Brigade.

The third tower to occupy its site, the memorial was inaugurated in 1923 and on the first Sunday in July it looks down on past and present members of the 45th and 95th of Foot, assembled in pilgrimage.

Homage of a different kind is paid at Crich from March to October by devotees of that clanking leviathan of municipal passenger transport, the tram. Here, at the National Tramway Museum based in a former quarry and utilising the quarrymen's old tramway, you can take a two-mile tram ride and inspect a 50-strong fleet which includes rolling stock from Prague, Blackpool and Edinburgh, spanning the period from 1873 to 1953 with traction ranging from electricity and steam to a horse-drawn tram of 1874.

The imagination which conceived this museum is also evident in the reconstruction of the façade of Robert Adam's Derby Assembly Rooms, ravaged by fire some years ago and later demolished. This now overlooks a trundle of trams resplendent in their distinctive livery. Happily, Crich has found a home for both of them.

Hardwick Hall

Behind the formidable façade of Hardwick Hall, near Chesterfield, lies the story of a no less formidable woman: Elizabeth de Hardwick, better known simply as Bess of Hardwick, who was born about 1520 at the now ruinous Hardwick Old Hall, a minor manor house.

At 13 she married a young landowner who soon died, leaving her an estate which gave her an income from lead-mining. At 27, she became the third wife of the statesman Sir William Cavendish, persuading him to sell his Suffolk estates and buy Chatsworth.

It was now that the ruling passion of her life began to become evident. Bess was addicted to building. Once she started, she couldn't stop.

First, she created a new Chatsworth House, an Elizabethan pile almost as large as the subsequent replacement we know today. Then Sir William died, leaving her wealthy enough to have no trouble finding a third husband, a knight who died less than a decade later.

In 1568 she shrewdly married the sixth Earl of Shrewsbury, who found her sweet enough at first. Sixteen years later, he was calling her evil and burdensome. She was certainly a schemer – she arranged marriages between two of Shrewsbury's children and two of her own, thus keeping the Shrewsbury/Cavendish wealth in the family. Her burdensome aspect was the expense of her building mania. Not content with Chatsworth, which put a strain on even her husband's pocket, she began building on his Worksop estate. When he complained, she told him he was a knave, a fool and a beast, and in 1583 they separated.

Excluded from Chatsworth, Bess turned to extending the small manor in which she was born. Then, with the Earl's death in 1590, she was freed from the constraints his lawyers had placed on her. Now 71, she celebrated by building a new Hardwick Hall, on a site near the old one.

It was completed in six years: a masterpiece of uncompromising, four-square unity crowned at intervals along the balustrades with Bess's initials, a nice touch of egocentric exuberance.

The extensive glazing, unusual at that time, prompted the rhyme, 'Hardwick Hall, more window than wall'. Within, Bess hung Flemish tapestries which are there to this day, together with other needlework for which the house is celebrated.

She enjoyed her new home for ten years before her death at 87. I wonder what she would have thought of the coming of age party held here for the sixth Duke of Devonshire in 1811, a high-spirited affair at which two guests were accidentally killed and the drunken were said to have sprawled around the park 'like the slain on a battlefield'.

Hardwick Hall subsequently became one of the Devonshires' dower houses, its last family occupant being the present Duke's grandmother. Now it is in the care of the National Trust, whose cleaning of the stonework has transformed a once sombre exterior into the gleaming sandstone that greets visitors today.

Belper

The name of this town is said to stem from 'Beau Repaire' – indicating its picturesque setting on the banks of the Derwent (*opposite*). Then industry came. It was water-power the factory-owners wanted, and never mind the scenery. Other towns could have their cathedrals: Belper would have mills – cathedrals of commerce.

Ironically it was the river Derwent, the feature which made the place so scenic, that was the attraction for the industrialists. So Beau Repaire was destroyed by its own beauty.

Had none of this happened, Belper would doubtless today be part of every tourist's itinerary. But in depriving the town of much of its visual appeal, the mill-owners gave Belper something else: prosperity, and a place in·industrial history.

In the late 18th century, Belper expanded swiftly to become a Derbyshire boom-town, the third largest centre of population in the county. Pre-eminent in bringing this about was Jedediah Strutt, who in 1759 invented a revolutionary process for making ribbed stockings.

He wasn't a Belper man – he came from South Normanton, near Alfreton – but it was Belper that he chose in 1776 as the site for his principal mills. In 1771

he had joined forces with Richard Arkwright, inventor of a machine for spinning cotton, to open the world's first successful water-powered cotton spinning mill at Cromford. Now he was to turn Belper into a mill town, and where he led, others followed.

With the decline of the textile industry today's Strutt Mill of 1912 is occupied by several firms engaged in a variety of businesses – a development mirrored by many another mill in Lancashire.

Sudbury Hall and Doveridge

In poor weather the thoughts of many turn to such indoor recreations as stately-home visiting, but take warning: don't go to Sudbury Hall on a dull day. Not if the hall's plasterwork, perhaps its principal glory, is what you wish to see. Good light is necessary for the appreciation of Sudbury Hall's ceilings. The 17th century artist-craftsmen responsible were London's Bradbury and Pettifer, and their work is magnificent. Vying with it for attention are the equally impressive skills of the woodcarvers Grinling Gibbons and Edward Pierce.

Until comparatively recently, the hall was a paradox. It was one of Derbyshire's best-known, least-known stately homes. You saw it simply by driving past, so close is it to a main road; but you couldn't see inside. Passers-by had been familiar with it since it began taking shape in the early 17th century, but it was not until the late 1960s that it became a National Trust property and was opened to the public.

From outside, the diamond-patterned mellow brickwork and ornate two-storey porch with cupola are the only hints of the richness to be found within what otherwise appears to be a country house modest by the standards of Chatsworth, Kedleston or Hardwick. Inside, however, Sudbury Hall is every bit as satisfying.

Nearby, at Doveridge, the parish church is noted for the breadth of its 13th century chancel and nave, its yard distinguished by an ancient yew and attendant canopy formed with another yew tree. The trunk of what has become known as the Doveridge Yew is well over 20 feet in girth, and with the church it stands in what were formerly the grounds of Doveridge Hall, demolished nearly half a century ago. The church's spire (*inset*) is seen from the meadows below the village.

Repton

This is where the writers Christopher Isherwood, Roald Dahl, Edward Upward and Vernon Watkins attended public school; and where two headmasters, William Temple and Geoffrey Fisher, went on to become successive Archbishops of Canterbury. But over the centuries, Repton has come down in the world. Now little more than a village best known for its school, it was once the capital of a kingdom.

From here in the seventh century the pagan King Penda ruled the Midland kingdom of Mercia. Penda's son married a Christian princess from Northumberland. With her came four priests, one of whom became the first Bishop of Mercia, founding a monastery at Repton.

Danes destroyed the abbey and its church in 875, but a new church, Saint Wystan's, was built a century later, followed in 1172 by an Augustinian priory, remnants of which survive today as part of Repton School.

Established in 1557, the school is approached through what was formerly the gateway of the priory, which was dissolved in 1538. Other portions of the priory became incorporated in the school's headmaster's house and its library and museum, but most of the school's premises are 19th and early 20th century.

It is for 10th century St Wystan's – named after a murdered prince – that Repton is architecturally most significant. Its crypt – the burial-place of royalty – and its chancel were noted by Pevsner as 'one of the most precious survivals of Late Saxon architecture in England'.

Nearer our own time, Repton is architecturally notable for Easton House (1907), one of the very few Derbyshire examples of the work of Edwin Lutyens. His client was a Repton School housemaster.

Pictured here are the school's priory gateway and, (*inset*), St Wystan's church, seen from a backwater of the river Trent.

Swarkeston Bridge and Shardlow Marina

Three important events in the county's history have links with the pictures on these pages. At Swarkeston Bridge in 1643 Sir John Gell's Roundheads routed Royalists trying to hold this key crossing of the Trent, and the bridge was the southernmost point reached by Bonnie Prince Charlie's advance guard in 1745. Dating from the 13th century, it is nearly three-quarters of a mile long, the greater part a causeway crossing fields prone to flooding – tradition says it was created by two sisters whose lovers drowned while trying to cross the submerged meadows. Today's bridge-proper is a rebuilding of 1802.

In 1777 the county's first canal, a stretch of the Trent and Mersey, was completed, followed by eight more Derbyshire inland waterways. These owed their creation primarily to the increasing demand for coal,

conveyed by canal far more cheaply than by the roads of the day. And the father of Britain's inland waterways was a Derbyshire man: James Brindley, from Tunstead.

The Trent and Mersey canal – originally called the Grand Trunk, England's first coast-to-coast waterway – was one of his creations, and at Shardlow (*inset*) it joins the navigable river Trent. The village thus became an inland port, with wharves and warehouses to accommodate cargo in transit. The Shardlow-based Cavendish Bridge Boat Company had 20 narrow boats on the canal by 1780, and the population of Shardlow nearly trebled in 40 years, peaking at 1,306 in 1841.

The Trent and Mersey reduced the cost of transporting goods from Manchester to Lichfield from an estimated £4 to £1 per ton, and the price of Lancashire coal was halved for Derbyshire users. But with the virtual demise of waterborne freight in the 1950s, Shardlow needed a new role, and in 1975 it found one with the development of a marina. The pleasure-cruising trail had been blazed, however, as long ago as 1774, when a family of eight completed a 15-day canal trip at Shardlow's Cavendish bridge, having covered 284 miles by water and 170 by land.

Although the canal basin has lost the bustle of its heyday, the gaily-painted narrow boats now lining its wharves ensure that it is no less colourful, particularly at weekends. I wonder what the Shardlow bargees of long ago would make of it all: in 1839, 140 of them petitioned the canal's owners to close the waterway on Sundays . . .

Melbourne Hall

Here is a house upstaged by its gardens. Behind its elegant 18th century façade, Melbourne Hall is something of a hotchpotch of various periods, more interesting for its historical associations than for its architecture. Its gardens, however, are another matter. They were laid out at the beginning of the 18th century by the royal gardeners, George London and Henry Wise, in the style of the grounds designed by André Le Notre for Louis XIV at Versailles. In addition to a yew tunnel 180 feet in length, they contain the *pièce de résistance* of the Derby ironsmith Robert Bakewell: an ornamental arbour (*opposite*) in the form of a domed cage, dating from the first decade of the 18th century.

And the historical associations? In the 17th century, Melbourne Hall was the home of Sir John Coke, who left the county in a hurry after Charles I sacked him from his position as the principal Secretary of State – his puritan inclinations were not to the monarch's taste, and Coke became a target for royalist harassment. The house was later owned by Queen Victoria's first prime minister, Viscount Melbourne, after whom the Australian city of Melbourne was named. The second Viscount Melbourne married the writer Lady Caroline Lamb, better known for her infatuation with Lord Byron than for her novels. Another Melbourne Hall literary link is to be found in the pages of George Eliot's *The Mill on the Floss*: at times of stress, the novel's Mrs Glegg finds comfort by reading *The Saint's Everlasting Rest* . . . written by the Nonconformist minister Richard Baxter, who used the Hall as a retreat.

The village of Melbourne is notable for its parish church, which has one of the finest Norman interiors in England. Of Melbourne's 14th century castle only a wall now remains – some of the castle's stones went into a 17th century extension of Melbourne Hall. It was at this fortress that the Duke of Bourbon was imprisoned, following his capture at Agincourt. Languishing there for 19 years he doubtless dreamt of going home . . . but this was four centuries before Melbourne became the birthplace of a man who could have made the necessary arrangements: Thomas Cook, the pioneer travel agent.

Calke Abbey

Imagine a stately home – the second largest in Derbyshire – where motor vehicles and bicycles were not allowed past the gates until 1924; electricity was not installed until 1962; a tunnel was bored under the grounds so that staff could go about their work without intruding on the scene; and a magnificent four-poster bed delivered in 1734 was not unpacked for more than two centuries.

None of this is fantasy. It is just part of the story of one of the most extraordinary houses of this or any other county: a home in which, for more than a century, little if anything was ever thrown away. When a room became full, the occupants simply closed it and moved to another.

Completed in 1703, Calke Abbey was the home of the Harpur Crewes, a family remarkable for a recurring reclusiveness. This first manifested itself in the 1730s. It sometimes skipped a generation or two, when life at Calke became relatively normal, but it invariably returned, one head of the family after another finding himself unable to communicate except by letter.

Sir Vauncey Harpur Crewe (1846-1924) achieved a degree of aristocratic eccentricity equalled in the county only by Renishaw Hall's Sir George Sitwell (1860-1943), whose wife was jailed because he wouldn't settle her debts – instead he spent a fortune on restoring an Italian castle occupied by 297 peasants, and otherwise devoted his time to inventing a toothbrush that played 'Annie Laurie', a revolver for shooting wasps and a synthetic square egg.

Stuffed birds were Sir Vauncey's obsession. He amassed thousands, and such was his dislike of society that when his wife received visitors, he hid in the grounds. When he caught one of his daughters smoking, he banished her from the house for the rest of his life; and when a cousin who was also a tenant displeased him, he had the man's home demolished.

But it is thanks primarily to Sir Vauncey's regime that Calke Abbey became the 'time-capsule' it is today, attracting many visitors in its new role as a National Trust property.

Derby

Where was the Rolls-Royce Silver Ghost built? Where was Samuel Johnson married? Where did the first Astronomer Royal go to school?

The answer in each case is Derby. When it became a city in 1977, there were those who were surprised to learn that it wasn't one already. For this is the home of such household names as Qualcast and Royal Crown Derby, and it has long been a major centre of the railway industry and the principal base of Rolls-Royce aero engines.

Derby Arboretum, opened in 1840, is claimed to be Britain's first municipal park, but in fact that distinction belongs to Preston, where Moor Park was created six years earlier. Derby, however, went on to become particularly well-endowed with parkland – residents on the north side of the city have the choice of three large parks, all within a short walk.

On the pioneering front, the city also had Britain's first viable silk mill; in the 1760s the artist Joseph Wright of Derby was the first in Britain to produce what became known as 'candlelight' paintings, with two celebrated pictures portraying scientific experiments; and, for connoisseurs of the esoteric, it was in Derby in 1878 that a local newspaper editor and a friend played the first game of chess to be conducted by telephone.

It is for something else, however, that every schoolchild knows of Derby, at least by name, for it was here in 1745 that Bonnie Prince Charlie's invading army ran out of steam and began its ill-fated retreat.

Other events in Derby's history include the hanging, drawing and quartering of three Catholic priests in 1588; the imprisonment of the Quakers' founder, George Fox, in 1650; the establishment of the Royal Crown Derby china works in 1748, continuing a local tradition of pottery manufacture dating back to the Roman occupation; and the arrival of Henry Royce (*inset*) in 1908, dedicated to building the best cars in the world, which continued to be manufactured in Derby until the motor division of Rolls–Royce moved to Crewe in 1946.

Kedleston Hall

People come to this 18th century Palladian house to savour England's best-preserved sequence of Robert Adam interiors, to see relics of the Raj or simply to be overawed. None of these quests is disappointed.

Visitors step over the south front's threshold into the Great Hall, which is precisely that. Forty feet high, flanked by towering alabaster columns, it seems to have been designed to make newcomers feel small. For Samuel Johnson, the whole house was over the top – 'It would do excellently,' he said, 'for a town hall'. Despite its no-expense-spared grandeur, there is something uncompromisingly austere about it ... as there was about George Curzon, who in 1898 became Baron Curzon of Kedleston and Viceroy of India – hence the Hall's Raj relics, echoes of a life-style which prompted Curzon's wife to write home: 'We might as well be monarchs'.

Curzon had a superiority complex because he *was* superior, intellectually and socially, to most of those around him ... although he never lost the Derbyshire accent he acquired during his upbringing by servants.

'No woman of the lower class has ever been able to attract him', noted the romantic novelist Elinor Glyn, with whom he had an affair after the death of his vicereine. And no woman was allowed to impede his career. His beautiful first wife had to wait five years, rejecting other suitors, until he found it convenient to marry her. 'Give me a girl who knows a woman's place and does not yearn for trousers', he told her. She knew he must always do as he wished, she assured him.

Kedleston had been his family home since the 12th century, and when he took his bride there in 1895 after their wedding in Washington DC, a special one-coach train conveyed the couple to Derby, where they were met by Curzon's father, the fourth Baron Scarsdale, and a line-up of aldermen. As church bells rang, two barouches took the party through crowd-flanked streets decorated with bunting, and out through the country to nearby Kedleston. At the Hall's gates, 40 tenants on horseback waited to escort the barouches up the drive to the house, where more than 500 tenants welcomed the couple with a formal message of greeting presented on a silver salver.

As things turned out, Curzon's bride didn't take to her father-in-law or to Kedleston's servants. But, American millionaire's daughter though she was, don't tell me she wasn't impressed when she stepped into that vast entrance hall.